Our Bodies

Our Brains

Charlotte Guillain

Heinemann
LIBRARY

www.heinemannlibrary.co.uk
Visit our website to find out more
information about Heinemann
Library books.

To order:

☎ Phone +44 (0) 1865 888066

🖹 Fax +44 (0) 1865 314091

🖳 Visit www.heinemannlibrary.co.uk

Heinemann Library is an imprint of Capstone Global Library Limited, a
company incorporated in England and Wales having its registered office at 7
Pilgrim Street, London, EC4V 6LB – Registered company number: 6695582

Heinemann is a registered trademark of Pearson Education Limited, under
licence to Capstone Global Library Limited

Text © Capstone Global Library Limited 2010
First published in hardback in 2010
The moral rights of the proprietor have been asserted.

Edited by Siân Smith, Laura Knowles, Nancy Dickmann, and
Rebecca Rissman
Designed by Joanna Hinton-Malivoire
Original Illustrations © Capstone Global Library Ltd. 2010
Illustrated by Tony Wilson
Picture research by Ruth Blair and Mica Brancic
Production by Duncan Gilbert and Victoria Fitzgerald
Originated by Capstone Global Library Ltd
Printed and bound in China by Leo Paper Group

ISBN 978 0 431 19509 4
14 13 12 11 10
10 9 8 7 6 5 4 3 2 1

British Library Cataloguing in Publication Data
Guillain, Charlotte.
  Our brains. -- (Acorn. Our bodies)
  1. Brain--Juvenile literature.
  I. Title II. Series
  612.8'2-dc22

Acknowledgements
We would like to thank the following for permission to reproduce
photographs: Corbis pp.**4** (© Tim Pannell), **10** (© Solus-Veer), **14** (©
LWA-Dann Tardif/zefa), **17** (© Roy Morsch/zefa), **20** (© Fancy/Veer), **22**
(© Tim Pannell); iStockphoto pp.**12**, **19** (© Mark Kalkwarf), **21** (© Julián
Rovagnati), **23** (© Mark Kalkwarf); Photolibrary pp.**5** (© Goodshoot), **8** (©
Glow Images), **9** (© White), **13** (© Glow Images), **15** (© Banana Stock), **16**
(© Corbis), **18**, **23** (© Asia Images); Science Photo Library p.**11** (© Geoff
Tompkinson).

Front cover photograph of children doing a jigsaw puzzle reproduced with
permission of Corbis (© Randy Faris). Back cover photograph reproduced
with permission of Photolibrary (© Corbis).

Every effort has been made to contact copyright holders of material
reproduced in this book. Any omissions will be rectified in subsequent
printings if notice is given to the publishers.

Community Learning & Libraries
Cymuned Ddysgu a Llyfrgelloedd

This item should be returned or renewed by the
last date stamped below.

ENRICHING
LEARNING IN
NEWPORT
SCHOOLS

Contents

Body parts

Our bodies have many parts.

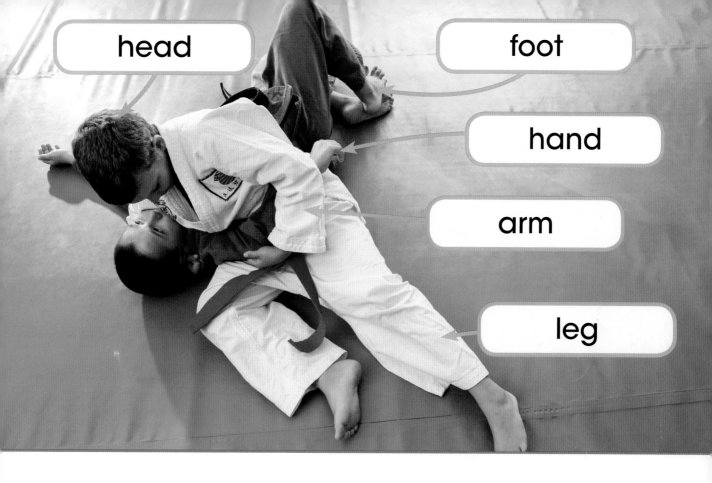

head

foot

hand

arm

leg

Our bodies have parts on
the outside.

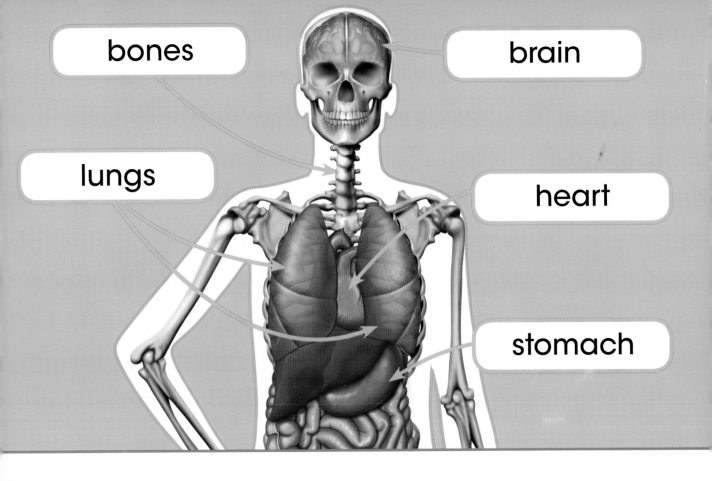

bones

brain

lungs

heart

stomach

Our bodies have parts on the inside.

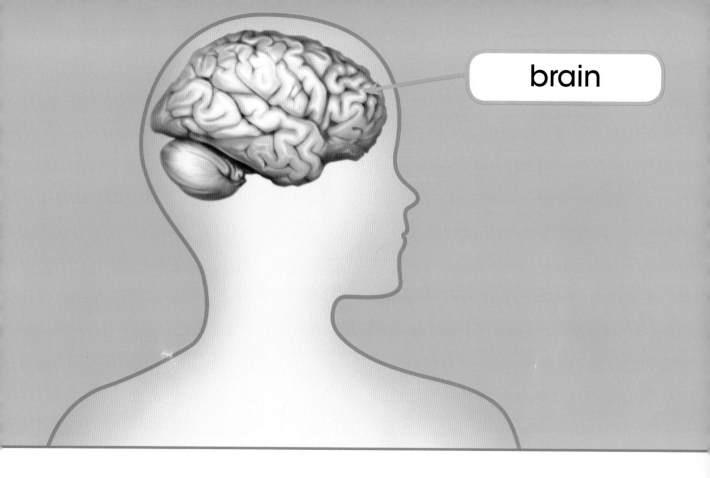

brain

Your brain is inside your body.

Your brain

You cannot see your brain.

head

Your brain is inside your head.

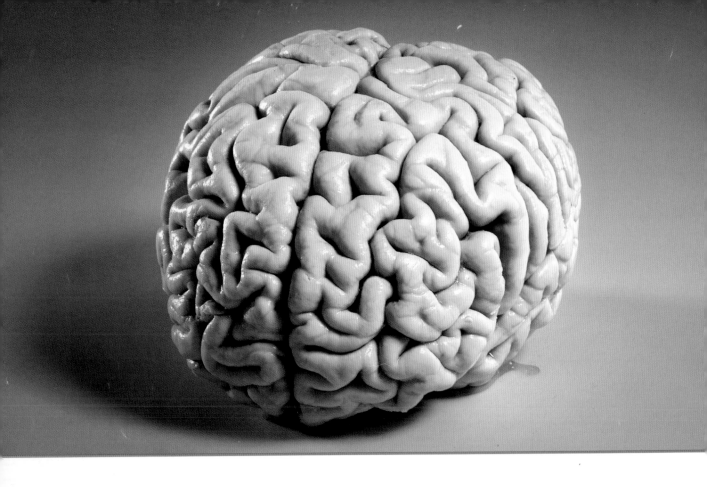

Your brain is wrinkly.

Your brain is soft.

Your working brain

Your brain tells your body what to do.

Your brain tells your body how to do things.

Your brain works when you
are thinking.

Your brain works when you
are moving.

Your brain works when you
are listening.

Your brain works all the time.

Staying healthy

You can get a lot of rest to help your brain.

You can do puzzles to help
your brain.

You can eat healthy food to help your brain.

You can drink a lot of water to help your brain.

Quiz

Where in your body is your brain?

Answer on page 24

Picture glossary

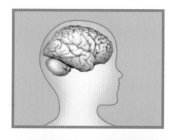

brain part of your body inside your head. You think with your brain. Your brain tells your body what to do.

puzzle game that gives you a problem to work out

rest to take time to relax and not do very much

Index

Answer to quiz on page 22: Your brain is in your head.

Notes to parents and teachers
Before reading
Ask the children to name the parts of their body they can see on the outside. Then ask them what parts of their body are inside. Make a list of them together and see if the children know what each body part does, for example, food goes into their stomachs. Discuss where their brain is and see if anyone knows what our brains do.

After reading
Play a memory game. Put the children into groups and give each group a tray, a cloth, and ten small objects. Demonstrate the game by showing them ten objects on a tray and then covering the tray with a cloth. Remove one object without the children seeing and then remove the cloth and ask them which object is missing. Then ask them to play the game in their groups, taking it in turns to hide the objects and remove one.

PILLGWENLLY

26-07-18